START TO Quilt

All the Basics PLUS Learn-to-Quilt Projects

Creative Publishing international
international
Chanhassen, Minnesota

Copyright © 2005
Creative Publishing international
18705 Lake Drive East
Chanhassen, Minnesota 55317
1-800-328-3895
www.creativepub.com
All rights reserved

Creative Publishing
international

President/CEO: Ken Fund

START TO QUILT

Created by: The Editors of Creative Publishing
international

Library of Congress Cataloging-in-Publication Data

Start to quilt : all the basics plus learn-to-quilt
projects / by the editors of Creative Publishing
International.

    p. cm.

  ISBN 1-58923-211-9 (soft cover)

 1. Quilting. 2. Patchwork. I. Creative Publishing
International.

TT835.S6876 2005
746.46--dc22

              2005006051

Printed in China
 10 9 8 7 6 5 4 3 2

The content of this book has been excerpted from
Quilting 101, published by Creative Publishing
international.

Due to differing conditions, materials, and skill levels,
the publisher and various manufacturers disclaim any
liability for unsatisfactory results or injury due to
improper use of tools, materials, or information
in this publication.

CONTENTS

HOW TO USE THIS BOOK

Refer to the **Quick References** at the right side of the pages for definitions or elaborations on any words or phrases printed *like this* on the page. If the word or phrase is followed by a page number, its reference can be found on the page indicated. Words printed **LIKE THIS** can be found in the **Glossary** on page 64.

Quilting SUPPLIES

The process of quilting involves several basic tasks: measuring, cutting, marking, and stitching. For each of these steps there are special tools and supplies to save you time, improve your accuracy, and make the project go smoothly.

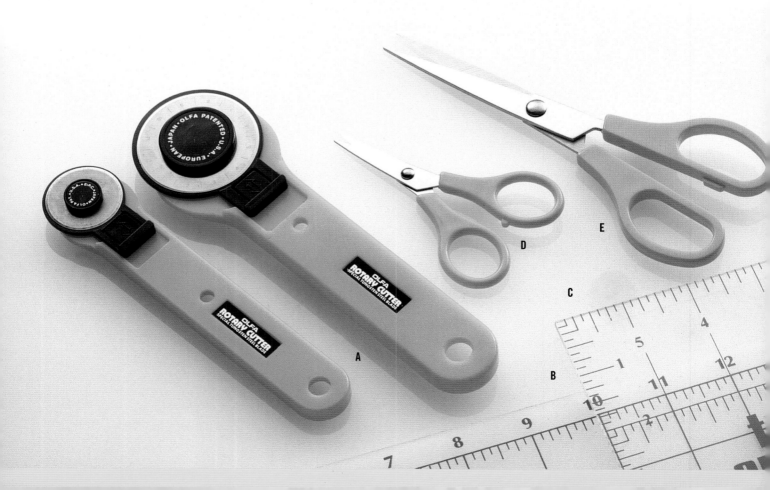

MEASURING & CUTTING TOOLS

Buy quality cutting tools and use them only for sewing! Cutting paper and other non-fabric materials will dull your tools quickly. Sharp tools make precise cuts easier and, in the long run, will save you time.

Rotary cutters **(A)** allow you to cut smooth edges on multiple layers of fabric quickly and easily. The cutters are available in different sizes. Small cutters work well for curves and a few layers of fabric; the larger ones are ideal for long straight lines and many layers of fabric.

Cutting mats **(B)**, made especially for use with rotary cutters, protect your blade and table top. Mats come in a variety of sizes. Choose one at least 22" (56 cm) wide to accommodate a width of fabric folded in half. A mat with a printed grid is a useful guide for cutting right angles.

You'll want a clear quilting ruler **(C)** to use as a measuring tool and as a guide for your rotary cutter.

A ruler 6" × 24" (15 × 61 cm) is a popular, versatile size. Square rulers and rulers with 30°, 45°, and 60° angle lines also are available.

Sewing scissors **(D)** and shears **(E)** are sewing necessities. Purchase the best quality you can afford.

MARKING TOOLS

The marks you make on fabric should last only as long as you need them. You should be able to remove them easily without damaging the quilt. Always test a marker on a sample swatch of fabric first and remember to mark lightly!

A special fabric eraser **(F)** can be used to remove light lead pencil marks without damaging fabric. Quilter's pencils **(G)**, available in white or gray lead, have eraser ends for easy removal. The leads are oil-free and contain less graphite to prevent smearing. Soapstone pencils **(H)**, made of pressed talc, can be sharpened to a fine point and rubbed off or wiped with a damp cloth. Water-soluble pencils **(I)**, handy for marking on darker fabrics, can be removed with a damp cloth.

PINS, NEEDLES & THREAD

A Quilting pins, used for pinning your pieces together, are 1¾" (4.5 cm) long and have large glass heads.

B Curved, rustproof safety pins in 1" to 1½" (2.5 to 3.8 cm) size make quick work of basting your quilting projects.

C Milliner's needles with small, round eyes are preferred by quilters who want to hand-baste the layers together.

D Betweens are short needles with round eyes for sewing small hand-quilting stitches. Sharps, similar to betweens but slightly longer, are used for appliquéing and general hand sewing.

E Cotton-covered polyester threads and 100% cotton threads are available for machine and hand quilting. Hand-quilting threads have a polished glacé finish that provides abrasion resistance and prevents tangling and knotting; 100% cotton basting thread is also available.

F Fine monofilament thread can also be used for machine quilting, making the stitches less noticeable.

PRESSING EQUIPMENT & TECHNIQUES

Pressing at each stage of construction is the secret to perfect piecing. The general rule is to press each stitched seam before crossing it with another. Often you can sew the same seam in numerous sets before making the trip to the ironing board to press them all.

Pressing your seams carefully is crucial to your success, second only to accurate sewing of the ¼" (6 mm) seams. Use the tip of the iron, moving only in the direction of the **GRAINLINES**. Be especially cautious when pressing seams sewn on the **BIAS**. Careless pressing can distort the shape and size of your quilt project. Both **SEAM ALLOWANCES** are usually pressed together to one side or the other. Following the pressing plan in the project directions will help you produce a neat, precise design.

Use a steam/spray iron with a wide temperature range. Buy a dependable, name-brand iron. Because your iron will be left on and standing still for several minutes between pressing steps, avoid an iron with an automatic shut-off feature.

An ironing board provides a sufficient surface for pressing, but you may want to invest in a fold-out surface, such as the Spaceboard™, shown above. It has a cotton cover printed with a measured grid to help you press your pieces more accurately.

Fabric INFORMATION

After you have chosen a quilt design, it's time to select the fabric. This may seem like a difficult task at first, but consider it an adventure and have fun. This is the time to use your vision and creativity. Just as two painters can paint the same landscape and produce very different effects, your choice of patterns, colors, and the way you combine them will give each project your unique style.

Fabrics made of 100% cotton or cotton blends can be used. Both are available in a wide variety of patterns and colors, so you'll have plenty of options to choose from. Many quilters prefer using 100% cotton fabrics because they find them easier to sew, press, mark, and hand-quilt.

If you are shopping for your fabrics in a quilt shop, they will probably be arranged according to their colors or print types, and you'll rarely find fabric that is not pure cotton. In a general fabric store, you may find a section for quilting fabrics, but there are probably other suitable fabrics located elsewhere in the store. Be sure to check the labels for fiber content and care.

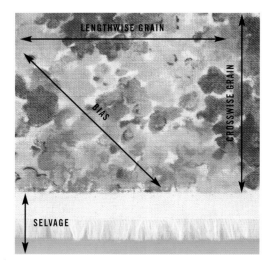

LENGTHWISE GRAIN

CROSSWISE GRAIN

BIAS

SELVAGE

FABRIC STRUCTURE

The outer edges of woven fabrics are called **SELVAGES**. As a general rule, they should be trimmed away (page 13), because they are more tightly woven than the rest of the fabric, and they may shrink when laundered or pressed. **GRAINLINES** are the directions in which the fabric yarns run. Strong, stable, lengthwise yarns, running parallel to the selvages, form the **LENGTHWISE GRAIN**. The **CROSSWISE GRAIN** is perpendicular to the lengthwise grain and has a small amount of give. The diagonal direction, which has considerable stretch, is called the **BIAS**.

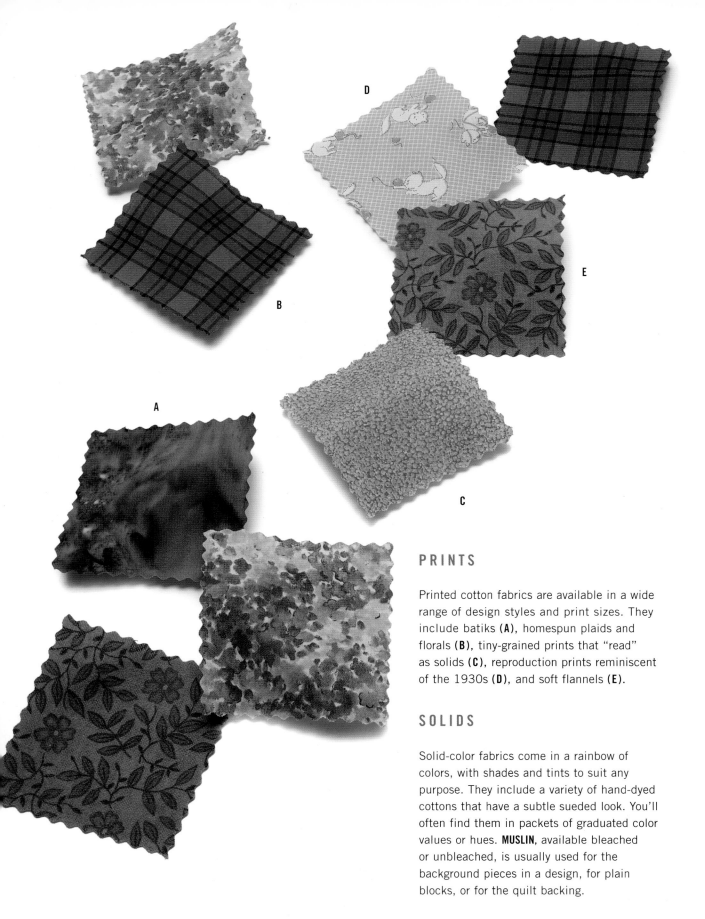

D

E

B

A

C

PRINTS

Printed cotton fabrics are available in a wide range of design styles and print sizes. They include batiks **(A)**, homespun plaids and florals **(B)**, tiny-grained prints that "read" as solids **(C)**, reproduction prints reminiscent of the 1930s **(D)**, and soft flannels **(E)**.

SOLIDS

Solid-color fabrics come in a rainbow of colors, with shades and tints to suit any purpose. They include a variety of hand-dyed cottons that have a subtle sueded look. You'll often find them in packets of graduated color values or hues. **MUSLIN,** available bleached or unbleached, is usually used for the background pieces in a design, for plain blocks, or for the quilt backing.

BACKING FABRICS

The backing fabric should have the same care requirements as the fabrics in the quilt top. For smaller projects, especially when the backing is visible, back the quilt top with one of the fabrics used on the front. For wall hangings and other items where the backing is rarely seen, muslin is a good choice. If you want to accentuate the quilting stitches on the backing side, choose a solid-colored fabric. Printed fabrics tend to hide the stitches.

PREPARING THE FABRIC

Preshrink your fabric, especially if you intend to launder the finished project. Most cotton fabrics shrink 2 to 3 percent when washed and dried, so if they're not preshrunk, the fabrics may pucker at the stitching lines and the finished size of the quilted piece may change the first time it is washed.

Launder fabrics in your washing machine on a short, warm cycle. There's no need to use detergent, but be sure to wash like colors together in case they aren't colorfast. Check the rinse water of dark or vivid fabrics to be sure they are colorfast; if dye transfers to the water, continue rinsing the fabric until the water is clear. Machine dry the fabric until it is only slightly damp, and then **PRESS** it.

SELECTING FABRICS

Use contrasting colors to make the pieces of a quilt block stand out from each other. Combine warm colors (reds, yellows, or oranges) in the same quilt block with cool colors (blues, greens, or violets) to make them all seem more vivid.

Left: Any fabric shape, whether solid-color or print, will "pop" from the quilt surface when surrounded by white or nearly white fabric.

Right: Select a multicolor print first, perhaps for the border. Then select fabrics for the quilt block pieces, drawing colors from the print.

Interesting visual effects are achieved by using colors with graduated values (lightness or darkness). Stack all the fabrics you are considering on a table; then stand back and squint. Or view them through a special filtering tool, available at quilt shops, designed for judging COLOR VALUES. The filter blocks out color and reveals only the intensity of the fabric.

Combine fabrics with various print scales and styles to add visual texture to your quilt. Don't be afraid to cut up a large-scale print into smaller pieces.

Rotary CUTTING

Accuracy in cutting is critical to successful quilting. A small error, multiplied by each piece, will result in blocks that don't fit together. You don't need that kind of frustration when you are learning to sew! Take the time to cut accurately, and give yourself a head start in the quilting game.

You'll find the investment in a rotary cutter and mat well worth it, once you start to use them. While indispensable for quilting, they are also perfectly suited for many other sewing projects. Rotary cutting is not only a very accurate method, it also saves time. Instead of cutting each piece of the quilt individually, you can cut several identical pieces at once and have the entire project cut and ready to sew in minutes.

STRAIGHTENING THE FABRIC

1 First, determine the **GRAINLINE**. Fold the fabric in half and hold it by the **SELVAGES**. Shift one side, if necessary, until the fabric hangs straight. The foldline is the straight **LENGTHWISE GRAIN**.

2 Lay the fabric on the cutting mat, with the fold along a grid line. Place the ruler on the fabric, close to the raw edge, at a 90º angle to the fold. Holding the ruler firmly in place with one hand, trim the excess fabric off along the edge of the ruler, using the rotary cutter. Apply steady, firm pressure to the blade. Stop when the rotary cutter gets past your hand.

3 Leave the blade in position, and reposition your hand on the ruler ahead of the blade. Hold firmly, and continue cutting. Make sure the fabric and the ruler don't move. Shift your hand position on the ruler whenever necessary.

4 Reposition the folded fabric on the cutting mat with the straightened end on a horizontal grid line. Place the ruler over the fabric perpendicular to the cut end, with the edge just inside the selvages. Cut off the selvages, using the rotary cutter as in steps 2 and 3.

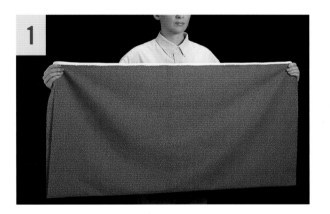

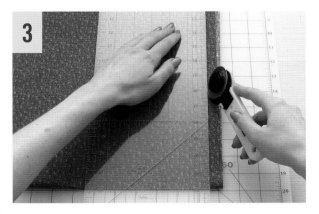

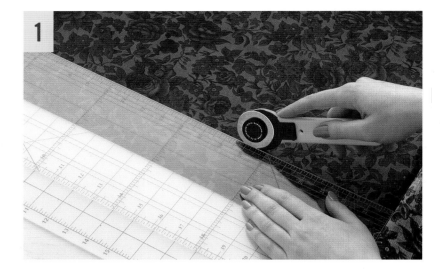

CUTTING STRIPS

1 Position the folded fabric so that the edge you will be cutting is on the left if you are right-handed, or on the right if you are left-handed. Place the ruler on the fabric, aligning the trimmed edge with the appropriate measurement on the ruler. Holding the ruler firmly, cut as on page 13, steps 2 and 3.

2 Lift the ruler and move the cut strip so that you are able to see the cutting line. Reposition the ruler and cut the next strip.

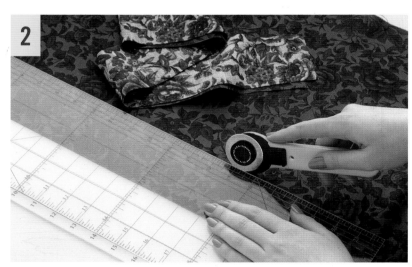

CUTTING SQUARES OR RECTANGLES

Stack three or four strips, matching the edges exactly. Place the ruler on the fabric, aligning the short edge of the fabric with the appropriate measurement on the ruler. Hold the ruler firmly in place. Cut the fabric, guiding the rotary cutter along the edge of the ruler.

TIP These photos show you how a right-handed person would hold the ruler and rotary cutter. If you are left-handed, you would hold the tools in opposite hands and work from the opposite direction.

CUTTING TRIANGLES

Stack three or four squares, matching the edges exactly. Place the ruler over the squares diagonally, aligning it exactly to the corners of the squares. Cut through the squares, guiding the rotary cutter along the edge of the ruler. The project directions will tell you what size to cut the squares and whether to cut them diagonally once or twice.

TIP Because rotary cutters are extremely sharp, the manufacturers have designed ways to cover or retract the blades. Always use this safety feature every time you put the tool down. An open blade falling from a table can easily slice through leather shoes. Keep your fingers out of the way when you are cutting, avoiding awkward positions where you have less control. Above all, keep the cutters in a safe place where children will not find them.

CUTTING A RECTANGLE WIDER THAN THE RULER

1 Measure the width of the strip in from the cut edge in several places; mark the fabric, using chalk or a pencil.

2 Align the ruler to the marks, and hold it firmly in place. Cut the fabric, guiding the rotary cutter along the edge of the ruler over the marks.

Quilt SEAMS

Quilting is like putting puzzles together. Lots of squares, rectangles, triangles, and fabric strips are pieced together to make a colorful fabric picture. Every **SEAM** is sewn using ¼" (6 mm) **SEAM ALLOWANCES**. In order to make all the pieces fit precisely, you must sew every seam accurately. Most machines have a seam allowance guide on the throat plate; however, it may not include a mark for ¼" (6 mm). Often, the distance from the needle tip to the edge of the presser foot is exactly ¼" (6 mm). If neither of these guides works for your machine, mark a ¼" (6 mm) seam guide on the bed of your machine with tape.

MAKING A SEAM GUIDE

Mark a line ¼" (6 mm) from the edge on a small square of fabric. Put the fabric under the presser foot, so that the marked line aligns to the tip of the needle. Place tape on the bed of the machine even with the cut edge of the fabric. Use the tape as a guide for sewing all your seams.

SEWING SEAMS

1 Thread your machine and insert the bobbin. Holding the needle thread with your left hand, turn the handwheel toward you until the needle has gone down and come back up to its highest point. A stitch will form, and you will feel a tug on the needle thread. Pull on the needle thread to bring the bobbin thread up through the hole in the throat plate. Pull both threads together under the presser foot and off to one side.

2 Place two fabric squares right sides together, aligning the outer edges. Pin the pieces together along one long edge, inserting the pins perpendicular to the edge. Place the fabric under the presser foot so the pinned side edges align to the ¼" (6 mm) seam guide and the upper edges align to the needle hole in the throat plate. Lower the presser foot, and set your stitch length at 2 mm, which equals 15 stitches per inch.

3 Begin stitching slowly. Hold the thread tails under a finger for the first few stitches. This prevents the needle thread from being pulled out of the needle and also prevents the thread tails

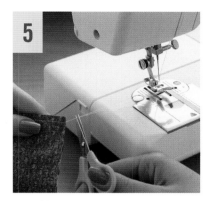

from being drawn down into the bobbin case, where they could potentially cause the dreaded *thread jam.* Gently guide the fabric while you sew by walking your fingers ahead of and slightly to the sides of the presser foot. Remember, you are only guiding; let the machine pull the fabric.

4 Stop stitching and remove pins as you come to them. When you reach the end of the fabric, stop again. Turn the handwheel toward you until the needle is in its highest position.

5 Raise the presser foot. Pull the fabric smoothly away from the presser foot, either to the left side or straight back. If you have to tug the threads, turn your handwheel slightly toward you until they pull easily. Cut the threads, leaving tails on the fabric and coming from the machine.

TIP Straight stitching lines are easier to achieve if you watch the edge of the fabric along the seam guide and ignore the needle. Sew smoothly at a relaxing pace, with minimal starting and stopping and without bursts of speed. You have better control of the speed if you operate your foot control with your heel resting on the floor.

QUICK REFERENCE

Thread jam. No matter how conscientious you are at trying to prevent them, thread jams just seem to be lurking out there waiting to mess up your day. **Don't use force!** Remove the presser foot, if you can. Snip all the threads you can get at from the top of the throat plate. Open the bobbin case door or throat plate, and snip any threads you can get at. Remove the bobbin, if you can. Gently remove the fabric. Thoroughly clean out the feed dog and bobbin area before reinserting the bobbin and starting over. Then just chalk it up to experience and get over it!

Selecting the BATTING

The middle layer of the quilt is called the batting. When selecting batting for any project, consider the amount of **LOFT**, its drapability, and the distance required between quilting stitches to prevent the batting from bunching or pulling apart. This distance, usually ranging from 1" to 6" (2.5 to 15 cm), is printed on the package label.

Cotton, polyester, and cotton/polyester blends are the most common fibers used in batting. Cotton batting gives a flat, traditional appearance when quilted. It absorbs moisture and is cool in the summer and warm in the winter. Polyester batting is more durable, is easier to handle than cotton, and gives a slightly puffier look. It provides warmth without weight, is nonallergenic, and resists moth and mildew damage. For the traditional appearance of cotton but the stability and ease in handling of polyester, choose a cotton/polyester blend.

Low-loft battings are recommended for machine quilting but even low-loft battings vary in thickness. Extra-low-loft battings are often used for garments or placemats. For wall hangings or lap quilts, select a low-loft batting that is sturdy but drapable.

Batting is available in a wide range of sizes, although the selection in certain fibers and construction types may be limited. Available in quilting stores and many fabric stores, batting can be purchased by the yard and in small packages for clothing and craft projects. It is also packaged for standard-size bed quilts.

Top: Low-loft polyester batting, used in this wall hanging, is easy to machine-quilt and very durable.

Middle: Cotton/polyester low-loft batting provides warmth, durability, and easy laundering for a cozy lap quilt.

Bottom: Extra-low-loft polyester batting is a good choice for placemats or table runners, when you want a subtle quilted look for an item that may be laundered often.

Layering and **BASTING**

Every quilt project, from the simplest one-piece hot pad to a multi-block bed quilt, must be layered and basted before you proceed with the actual quilting stitches. Basting keeps the quilt top, batting, and backing from shifting while you are quilting. Traditionally, quilts have been basted using a hand needle and thread. While this is still a viable alternative, you may save a little time basting with safety pins. If you prefer basting with thread, use a single strand of white cotton thread and a large milliner's or darning needle. For safety-pin basting, use only rustproof pins in either 1" or 1½" (2.5 or 3.8 cm) size. For either method, follow the same steps for layering the quilt.

LAYERING THE QUILT

1 **PRESS** the quilt top and
backing fabric flat. Mark the
center of each side of the quilt top
at the raw edges, using safety pins.
Repeat this step for the batting and
the backing. Place the backing on
your work surface, wrong side up.
Use masking tape to tape the
backing securely to your work
surface, beginning at the center of
each side and working toward the
corners. Keep the fabric taut but
not stretched.

2 Place the batting on the
backing, matching the center
pins on all sides. Smooth the
batting (but don't stretch it), working
from the center of the quilt out
to the sides.

3 Place the quilt top, right side
up, over the batting, matching
the pins on each side. Again,
smooth the fabric without stretching
it. For clarity, the photos show a
solid piece of fabric in place of a
multicolor pieced quilt top.

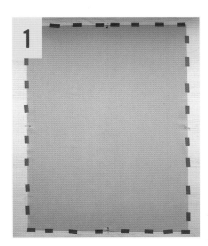

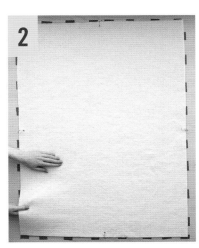

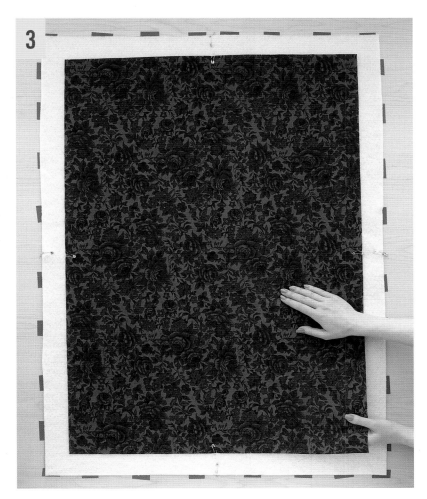

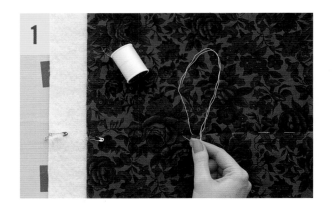

BASTING WITH THREAD

1 Thread the needle with a long strand of thread; tie a knot in the end. Begin at the center of the quilt, and stitch toward the side, taking 1" (2.5 cm) stitches through all three layers. Avoid stitching directly on seamlines or marked quilting lines. Pull the stitches snug so the layers will not shift.

2 Baste to the side of the quilt. *Backstitch* two or three stitches to secure.

3 Repeat steps 1 and 2 in each direction, so that you have divided the quilt into four quadrants with the basting stitches.

4 Baste parallel rows of stitches, no less than 6" (15 cm) apart, in one quadrant of the quilt. Work from the existing basting line toward the outer edge. Then repeat with parallel rows in the opposite direction.

TIP As you run out of thread, backstitch a few stitches. Then rethread the needle, knot the thread, and continue basting from where you stopped.

5 Repeat step 4 for each quadrant of the quilt. Remove the tape from the backing. Fold the edges of the backing over the batting and edges of the quilt top, and safety-pin them in place. This prevents the raw edges from raveling and prevents the batting from catching on the needle and feed dogs during quilting.

QUICK REFERENCE

Backstitch. Take a few stitches in the opposite direction when you get to the end of a basting row. This will hold the basting in place and is easier to remove than a knot.

BASTING WITH SAFETY PINS

Follow the same guidelines, first dividing the quilt into quadrants, and then working on one quadrant at a time. Insert all the pins in the same direction. Space them no more than 6" (15 cm) apart in parallel rows, vertically and horizontally. Avoid placing pins where you will be quilting.

TIP Safety-pin basting goes more quickly if the pins are all open. In fact, they can be purchased at quilting stores already opened. Then, as you remove them from your quilt, leave them open and ready for the next project. You'll save a little wear and tear on your fingers.

Basic Quilting TECHNIQUES

Quilting holds the quilt top, batting, and backing of the quilt together. But beyond its function, quilting adds texture and interest to the quilt, enhancing its pieced

design. For best effect, the quilting should reinforce or complement

the piecing or appliqué design, and it should form an appealing design on the back as

well as the front of the quilt.

You can quilt by hand or by machine; there are advantages to either method.

Hand quilting is the traditional method, and many quilters still prefer it that way.

Machine quilting, of course, takes less time and is also more durable. Whether

quilting by hand or machine, your stitching should cover the surface of the quilt

uniformly. This guideline is more than just an aesthetic consideration; heavily quilted

areas tend to shrink more than lightly quilted areas.

WHAT YOU'LL NEED

FOR HAND QUILTING:

Hand-quilting thread

Between or sharp hand
needle (page 6)

Thimble

Quilting hoop

FOR MACHINE QUILTING:

Walking foot

All-purpose thread or
nylon monofilament
thread

HAND QUILTING

1 Center the area you will work on in your **QUILTING HOOP.** Thread a between or sharp needle with a single strand of hand-quilting thread, about 18" (46 cm) long; tie a small knot in the end. Take one long stitch, inserting the needle from the front into the batting, about 1" (2.5 cm) from where you want to begin stitching. Don't stitch through to the backing. Bring the needle up where you will begin quilting.

2 Pull on your thread, gently "popping" the knot under the surface of the fabric. Don't pull too hard, or you'll pull the stitch out completely.

3 Take small, even stitches, up and down, through all three layers. If possible, take two to four stitches on your needle before pulling it through the quilt. Strive for quilting that looks the same on the front and the back of the quilt. The stitches should be the same length on both sides.

| TIP | To avoid poking a hole in the finger that pushes the needle, you'll want to wear a thimble. Many quilters find leather thimbles more comfortable than plastic or metal. |

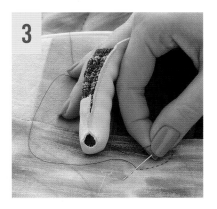

4 To finish a row of quilting, tie a small knot close to the surface of the fabric next to your last stitch. Use your thumbnail to gently pull the fabric, again "popping" the knot under the surface of the fabric. Take a shallow stitch, and clip the thread.

| TIP | While small stitches are desirable, uniformity is more important. Practice taking six stitches per inch (2.5 cm) as a beginner. |

4

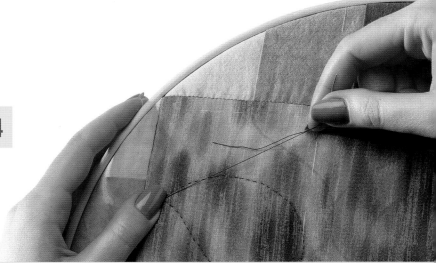

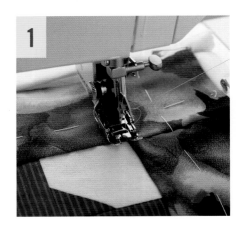

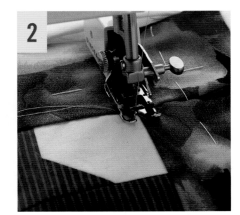

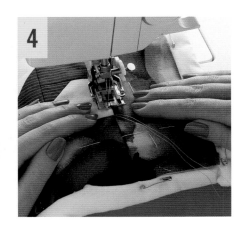

MACHINE QUILTING

1 Attach a walking foot. Place the quilt under the foot, in the area where you will begin quilting. Lower the foot. Turn the handwheel by hand for one stitch, and stop with the needle at the highest position. Raise the foot, and pull on the needle thread to bring the bobbin thread up through the fabric.

2 Draw both threads under the walking foot to one side. Lower the walking foot, with the needle aligned to enter the fabric at the desired starting point.

3 Stitch several very short stitches to secure the threads at the beginning of the stitching line. Gradually increase the stitch length for about 1/2" (1.3 cm), until it is about 15 stitches per inch, which equals 2 mm.

4 Slow your stitching as you approach a stopping point. Beginning about 1/2" (1.3 cm) from the end, gradually decrease the stitch length until you are barely moving, to secure the threads.

TIP Stitch with your hands positioned on either side of the walking foot, holding the fabric taut.

MACHINE-QUILTING PATTERNS

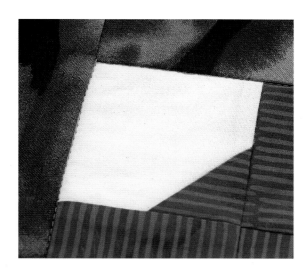

Stitch-in-the-ditch quilting emphasizes the pieced design because it is stitched following the seamlines for the blocks. Stitch so that the needle enters the well of the seam.

Outline quilting. Stitch about 1/4" (6 mm) away from the seamlines.

TIP Whenever you need to change direction, stop with the needle down in the fabric. Raise the walking foot, and **PIVOT**. Then lower the walking foot and continue stitching.

Channel quilting is stitched in relatively evenly spaced lines. You can mark them before you layer and baste the quilt or, for a less formal look, you can stitch them more irregularly. The quilting lines can be diagonal, vertical, or horizontal.

BINDING

Binding is the final step for most of your quilting projects. Enclosing the edges of the quilt, the binding forms a clean, attractive finish. Binding fabrics can either match or complement the other fabrics in the quilt. Very often a quilt is bound in the same fabric as the outer border.

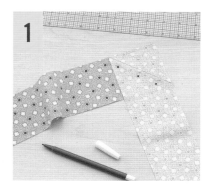

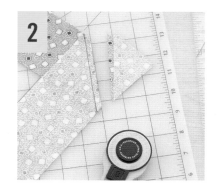

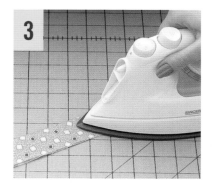

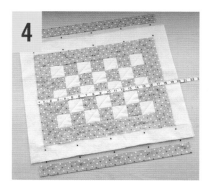

BINDING A QUILT

1 Cut 3" (7.5 cm) binding strips from the entire crosswise width of the fabric. If the sides of your quilt are shorter than the length of the binding strips, go on to step 3. If the sides of your quilt are longer than one binding strip, pin two strips, right sides together, at right angles. Mark a diagonal line from the corner of the upper strip to the corner of the lower strip. Stitch on the marked line.

2 Trim the **SEAM ALLOWANCES** to ¼" (6 mm). **PRESS** the seam open.

3 Press the binding strips in half lengthwise, wrong sides together.

4 *Measure the quilt top across the middle,* from side to side. Cut two binding strips equal to this measurement plus 2" (5 cm). Mark the binding strips 1" (2.5 cm) from the ends. Divide the length between the pins in fourths, and pin-mark. Also divide the upper and lower edges of the quilt in fourths, and pin-mark. CONTINUED

QUICK REFERENCE

Measure the quilt top across the middle. After piecing and quilting a quilt top, it is likely that the top and bottom may be slightly different lengths. By making both bindings the same length as the middle of the quilt, you are able to square up the finished project.

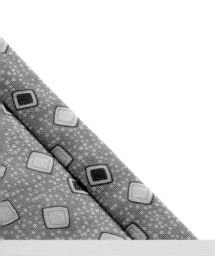

5 Pin a binding strip on the right side of the upper edge of the quilt, aligning the raw edges of the binding to the raw edge of the quilt top and matching the pin marks. *Insert the pins perpendicular to the raw edges.* The binding will extend 1" (2.5 cm) beyond the quilt at each end.

6 Stitch the binding strip to the quilt ¼" (6 mm) from the raw edges of the binding. *Remove the pins as you come to them.*

7 Trim off the excess batting and backing ½" (1.3 cm) from the stitching line.

8 Wrap the binding snugly around the edge of the quilt, covering the stitching line on the back of the quilt. Pin the binding in place from the right side, inserting the pins parallel to the binding in the seam "ditch" and catching the folded edge on the back.

TIP For easy removal, insert all the pins so that the heads will be toward you when you are stitching.

9 Stitch in the ditch (page 27) on the right side of the quilt, catching the binding on the back of the quilt. Remove the pins as you come to them.

10 Repeat steps 5 to 9 for the lower edge of the quilt. Trim the ends of the upper and lower binding strips even with the edges of the quilt top.

11 Repeat steps 4 to 7 for the sides of the quilt, measuring the quilt top down the middle, from top to bottom, in step 4. Trim the ends of the binding strips to extend ½" (1.3 cm) beyond the finished edges of the quilt.

12 Wrap and pin the binding around the edge, as in step 8. At each end, fold in the raw edges of the binding. Then fold under the ½" (1.3 cm) end; press. Finish wrapping and pinning the binding. Stitch the binding as in step 9.

QUICK REFERENCE

Insert the pins perpendicular to the raw edges. This makes it easier to remove them as you sew. The pin heads are near the raw edge where you can grasp them with your right hand. In this position, you are much less likely to stick yourself with a pin as you sew.

Remove pins as you come to them. As tempting as it may be, don't sew over pins! You may be lucky and save a few seconds, or you could hit a pin and break your needle, costing you much more time in the long run.

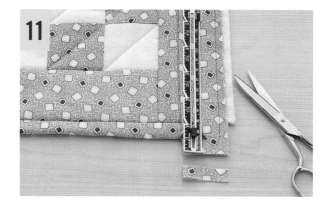

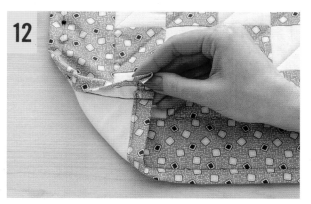

Raw-edge Appliqué HOT PAD

Raw-edge **APPLIQUÉS** add dimension and interest to a quilted project. Practice the technique by creating this maple leaf hot pad. Because the batting is quite thin, these hot pads are more decorative than useful. The edges of the leaf can be frayed with a stiff brush. For minimal fraying, use a tightly woven fabric for the appliqué. If you would like a more natural frayed look, machine wash and tumble dry the hot pad. The finished hot pad is about 9" (23 cm) square.

WHAT YOU'LL LEARN

How to sew a raw-edge appliqué

How to channel-quilt

How to bind the edge

WHAT YOU'LL NEED

⅜ yd. (0.35 m) background fabric, for the hot pad

¼ yd. (0.25 m) contrasting fabric, for the appliqué and binding

Low-loft batting, about 13" (33 cm) square

Rotary cutter and mat

Quilting ruler

Thread to match or blend with the fabrics

Glue stick

Decorative ring

How to Sew a **RAW-EDGE APPLIQUÉ HOT PAD**

LET'S BEGIN

1 Straighten the cut ends of the fabric, and trim off the **SELVAGES** (page 13). Cut a 9" (23 cm) square of background fabric for the hot pad front. Cut a 13" (33 cm) square of background fabric for the back. Cut a 13" (33 cm) square of batting. Cut four 3" × 11" (7.5 × 28 cm) strips of contrasting fabric for the binding. *Cut a leaf appliqué* from the contrasting fabric, about 6" (15 cm) wide.

2 *Glue-baste* the leaf appliqué, right side up, to the right side of the hot pad front. Position the leaf as desired in the center of the square.

3 Layer and baste the hot pad (page 20). Remove the layers from the work surface. Attach a walking foot, if you have one. Set your stitch length at 12 stitches per inch, which equals 2.5 mm. Begin stitching in the upper right corner of the pad, about 1" (2.5 cm) from the cut edge of the top layer.

4 Stitch from top to bottom, *stopping with the needle down in the fabric.* Lift the presser foot, **PIVOT** the hot pad 90°, and lower the presser foot. Stitch about 1" (2.5 cm). Stopping with the needle down, lift the presser foot, and pivot the hot pad another 90° to begin a new row of stitching. CONTINUED

QUICK REFERENCE

Cut a leaf appliqué. Draw a pattern freehand, or trace around a real leaf. Because the edges will not be finished in any way, avoid any long narrow extensions or small details that could ravel away entirely.

Glue-baste. Using a **GLUE STICK**, apply dots of glue to the wrong side of the appliqué. This will hold it temporarily in place until you catch it permanently to the hot pad with quilting stitches.

Stopping with the needle down in the fabric. Stop running the machine with the foot pedal. Turn the handwheel on your machine manually until the needle is all the way down into the fabric.

How to Sew a RAW-EDGE APPLIQUÉ HOT PAD

CONTINUED

5 Repeat this process until the entire hot pad is channel-quilted (page 27), catching the appliqué in the stitching. If you basted the hot pad with safety pins, remove them as you come to them.

TIP Relax! The rows of channel quilting don't need to be perfectly parallel. In fact, some variation is desirable to give it handmade charm.

6 Bind the edges of the hot pad, following the directions on page 28. Hand-stitch a small decorative ring to one corner, for hanging, if desired.

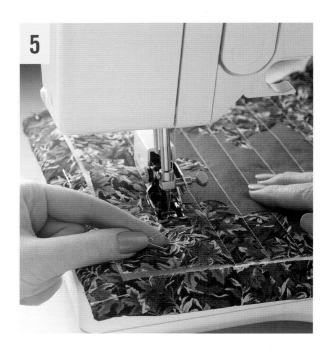

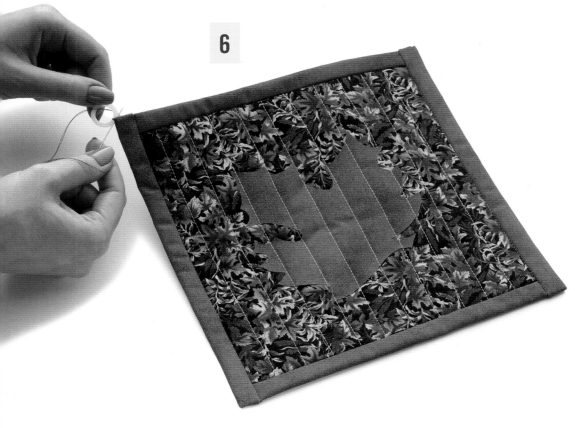

VARIATIONS ON THE THEME

Make hot pads for all seasons. Stitch a fir tree appliqué over a snowy print fabric for a winter hot pad. Get in the Halloween spirit with fall colors and a pumpkin appliqué. Or how about a spring fever hot pad?

Checkerboard PLACEMATS

Add homespun charm to your dining table with this set of four checkerboard placemats. Select two coordinating print fabrics, a print and a solid, or two solids, preferably with a high contrast between them.

The directions are for four placemats. You will find that this **STRIP-PIECING** method of construction saves time in sewing and cuts down on the number of trips back and forth to the ironing board. Set your machine for a straight stitch of 10 to 12 stitches per inch, which equals 2.5 mm, and sew ¼" (6 mm) **SEAM ALLOWANCES** throughout the entire project. Each placemat measures about 14" × 18" (35.5 × 46 cm).

WHAT YOU'LL LEARN

Strip piecing saves time

How to add a border to your quilt project

How to align seam intersections perfectly

WHAT YOU'LL NEED

½ yd. (0.5 m) light-colored print or solid fabric, we'll call "A"

2 yd. (1.85 m) darker-colored print or solid fabric, we'll call "B"

Low-loft polyester or poly/cotton blend batting

Rotary cutter and mat

Quilting ruler

Thread to match fabric A

How to Sew CHECKERBOARD PLACEMATS

1 Straighten the cut ends of the fabrics, and trim off the **SELVAGES** (page 13). Cut five 2½" (6.5 cm) strips from the entire crosswise width of fabric A. Cut five 2½" (6.5 cm) strips from the entire crosswise width of fabric B.

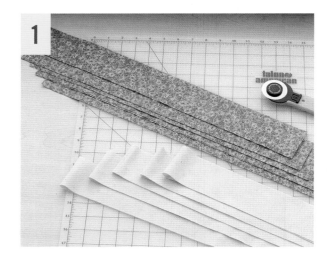

2 Cut seven 2½" (6.5 cm) strips from the entire crosswise width of fabric B, for the border. Cut seven 3" (7.5 cm) strips from the entire crosswise width of fabric B, for the binding.

3 Pin an A strip and a B strip right sides together, aligning the long edges; *insert the pins perpendicular to the long edge(p. 31).* Stitch the strips together, *removing the pins as you come to them (p. 31).* Then stitch another A strip to the other side of the B strip, in the same manner. Continue adding strips, alternating fabrics, until you have three A strips and two B strips. **PRESS** the seam allowances *toward the darker fabric* (B).

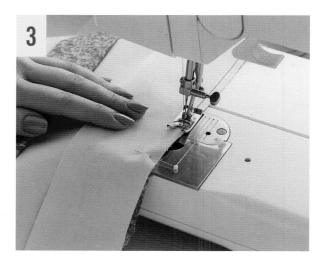

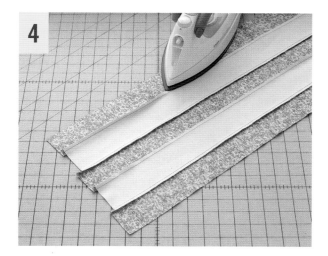

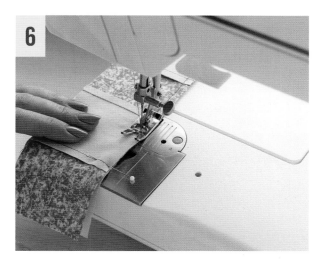

4 Stitch three B strips and two A strips together, as in step 3, with fabrics alternating in the opposite sequence. Press the seam allowances toward the darker fabric (B).

5 Cut the pieced strip sets, perpendicular to the seams, into 2½" (6.5 cm) strips.

TIP If your fabric is 45" (115 cm) wide, you should be able to cut at least 17 small strips from each set. You will need 16 strips of one set and 12 of the other to complete all four placemats.

6 Align the raw edges of two different strips, right sides together, matching the seams. The seam allowances will be pressed in opposite directions. *Insert a pin in the well of the seams,* to make sure they line up exactly. Stitch the strips together, removing the pins as you come to them and keeping the seam allowances turned in opposite directions. CONTINUED

QUICK REFERENCE

Toward the darker fabric. In piecing a quilt top, seam allowances are often pressed toward darker pieces to avoid show-through under light-colored pieces.

Insert a pin in the wells of the seams. By pinning in this manner, you are making sure that the stitched seams will line up perfectly on the right side. Stitch up to these pins as close as you can before removing them.

How to Sew CHECKERBOARD PLACEMATS

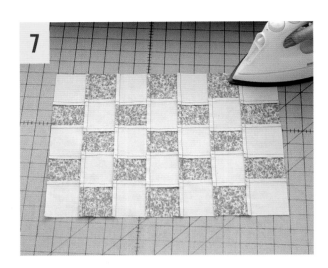

CONTINUED

7 Add five more strips as in step 6, alternating patterns, for a total of seven strips. Press all the new seam allowances in the same direction.

8 *Measure the placemat lengthwise across the middle (p. 29).* Cut two border strips equal to this measurement. Pin one strip to the top of the placemat; pin the other strip to the bottom. Align the ends of the strips to the sides of the placemat. Stretch the strips or the placemat slightly, if necessary, to make them fit. Stitch ¼" (6 mm) seams; press the seam allowances toward the borders.

9 Measure the placemat widthwise across the center, including the new borders. Cut two border strips equal to this measurement. Pin a strip to each side of the placemat, aligning the ends of the strips to the top and bottom edges of the placemat. Stretch the strips or the placemat slightly, if necessary, to make them fit. Stitch ¼" (6 mm) seams; press the seam allowances toward the borders.

10 Repeat steps 6 to 9 for the three other placemats. Cut the backing fabric and batting 4" (10 cm) longer and wider than the placemat. Layer and baste the placemats (page 20).

11 Attach a walking foot. Quilt by stitching in the ditch (page 27), *following this sequence:* Begin with a vertical seam near the center, then a horizontal seam near the center. Then stitch in the ditch of the seam between the border and pieced section. Finish by stitching the remaining vertical seams between rows and the remaining horizontal seams between rows. Bind each placemat, following the directions on page 28.

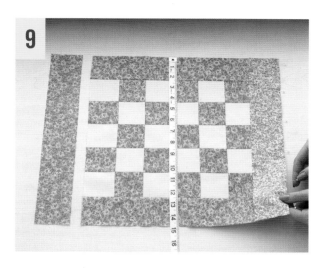

QUICK REFERENCE

Following this sequence. By quilting in this sequence, you first anchor the quilt vertically and horizontally, preventing the layers from shifting.

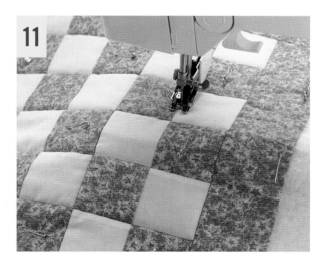

Pieced Sashing **TABLE RUNNER**

This table runner, with pieced **SASHING** and quilted motifs, will add a personal decorating touch to your dining room table. The motifs in the center of each square offer an opportunity to practice quilting by hand (page 25). The sashing is made of four hand-dyed fabrics with graduated **COLOR VALUES** from light to dark. These are often sold in quilt shops, already cut into pieces called **FAT QUARTERS**. Select a print fabric for the large center squares and the *connecting squares (p. 47)* of the sashing. Then select four graduating colors that accent the print.

The finished size is approximately 52" × 16" (132 × 40.5 cm). All **SEAM ALLOWANCES** for this project are ¼" (6 mm). Select machine-quilting thread in a color to match or blend with the fabrics; select hand-quilting thread (page 6) in a contrasting color.

WHAT YOU'LL LEARN

How to select and use fabrics in graduated color values

How to make pieced sashing

How to make your own **QUILTING TEMPLATE**

How to quilt by hand

WHAT YOU'LL NEED

2 yd. (1.85 m) printed fabric A for large blocks, connecting squares in sashing, backing, and binding

Four hand-dyed fabrics in fat quarters, or ¼ yd. (0.25 m) each of four full-width fabrics in graduated color values, for the sashing

Low-loft batting, about 56" × 20" (142 × 51 cm)

Rotary cutter and mat

Quilting ruler

Thread for machine quilting; thread for hand quilting

Between or sharp hand needle (page 6)

Heavy paper

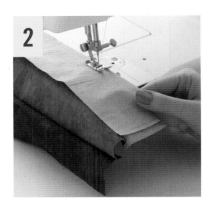

LET'S BEGIN

1 Straighten the cut edges of your fabrics, and trim off the **SELVAGES** (page 13). Cut four 8½" (21.6 cm) squares from fabric A; also cut ten 4½" (11.5 cm) squares from fabric A. Cut 2½" (6.5 cm) strips from the entire crosswise width of each of the remaining fabrics; you'll need four strips of each if they are fat quarters or two strips of each if they are 45" (115 cm) wide.

2 Arrange the strips of graduated colors in order from darkest to lightest. Place one strip from the first stack, right sides together, over a strip from the second stack, aligning the long edges. Stitch the strips together. Continue adding strips in graduated sequence from darkest to lightest.

TIP You can sew these strips together without pinning first if you take your time. Keep the edges aligned and hold both strips with even tension. The strips may not be exactly the same length. Start with the ends

evenly aligned and begin stitching from that same end with each additional strip.

3 Sew the remaining strips into sets like the first one. **PRESS** all the seam allowances *toward the darker fabric (p. 41).*

4 Cut the pieced fabric crosswise into 4½" (11.5 cm) strips. You will need a total of 13 pieced sashing strips.

5 Arrange all of the pieces on a flat surface, and step back for a long look. There are many ways you might turn the sashing strips, causing the gradation of color to change direction. You may prefer an arrangement different from the one we have selected.

6 Stitch the long outer rows of sashing strips and *connecting squares* together, keeping the pieces in their arranged order. Press the new seam allowances toward the connecting squares. Return the sashing units to the surface. CONTINUED

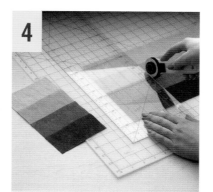

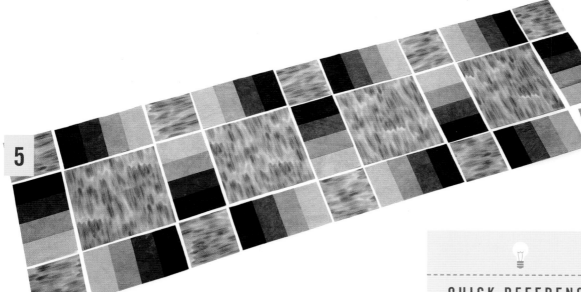

QUICK REFERENCE

Connecting squares. Sometimes sashing strips travel uninterrupted from one side of the quilt to the other. However, in this project, the sashing is made up of short pieces, alternating with contrasting squares. These squares "connect" pieces of the sashing in both directions, while adding an interesting design element to the overall pieced pattern of the table topper.

How to Sew a PIECED SASHING TABLE RUNNER

CONTINUED

7 Stitch the center row of sashing strips and large squares together, keeping the pieces in their arranged order. Press the new seam allowances toward the squares.

TIP Pin these pieces together first, one seam at a time, if you prefer. Stitch with the square on top, taking care to keep the seam allowances of the pieced strip turned in the direction they were pressed.

8 Place the bottom sashing row along the lower edge of the center row, with right sides together, matching the seams. The seam allowances will be pressed in opposite directions at the seam

intersections. *Insert a pin in the well of the seams (p. 41),* to make sure they line up exactly. Stitch the rows together, *removing the pins as you come to them (p. 31)* and keeping the seam allowances turned in the proper directions.

9 Stitch the remaining sashing row to the other side of the center row, as in step 8. Press these long seam allowances toward the center row.

10 Cut a quilting template of the desired shape from heavy paper, approximately 2½" (6.5 cm) tall and wide. Center the template in a connecting square. Trace lightly around the pattern, using a fabric marker (page 5). Repeat for each of the connecting

squares. Trace four intertwined motifs in each large square.

11 Cut the backing and batting 4" (10 cm) longer and wider than the table runner. Layer and baste the table runner (page 20). Quilt by machine, stitching in the ditch (page 27) of the lengthwise sashing seams and all the crosswise seams that run edge to edge. Use a walking foot.

12 Hand-quilt (page 25) over the marked motifs in each connecting square and in the large squares. Remove your basting stitches. Cut binding strips from fabric A, and bind the table runner (page 28).

9

10

11

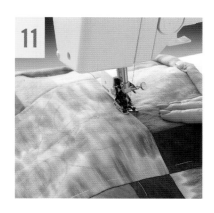

12

Rail Fence **WALL HANGING**

Rectangles can be found in dozens of block quilt designs. Here they're combined in the Rail Fence pattern to create a dynamic wall hanging. A light-to-dark progression of four fabrics accentuates the quilt's zigzag pattern. Select four small prints with **COLOR VALUES** that progress from dark to light. Or select two solids and two prints that give the same effect. A two-color border, using the two darkest fabrics, creates the illusion of a mat and frame.

All of the **SEAM ALLOWANCES** for this project are ¼" (6 mm). Sew as accurately as possible to ensure perfectly matched **SEAMS**. The finished size is about 38½" × 30½" (98 × 77 cm).

WHAT YOU'LL LEARN

STRIP-PIECING saves time

How to sew a quilt with a double border

How color arrangement creates optical illusions

WHAT YOU'LL NEED

⅜ yd. (0.35 m) fabric A (very light)

⅜ yd. (0.35 m) fabric B (light)

½ yd. (0.5 m) fabric C (medium)

1⅝ yd. (1.5 m) fabric D (dark)

1¼ yd. (1.15 m) of muslin, for backing

Batting, about 42" × 32" (107 × 81.5 cm)

Rotary cutter and mat

Quilting ruler

Thread

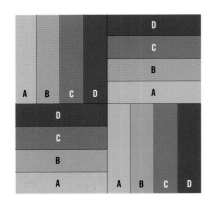

LET'S BEGIN

1 Straighten the cut ends of the fabric, and trim off the **SELVAGES** (page 13). Cut six 1½" (3.8 cm) strips from the entire crosswise width of each of the four fabrics. Arrange the strips in four stacks (A to D) according to their color value, from lightest to darkest.

2 Pin an A strip and a B strip right sides together, aligning the long edges; *insert the pins perpendicular to the long edge (p. 31)*. Stitch the strips together, *removing the pins as you come to them (p. 31)*. Then stitch a C strip to the other side of the B strip. Add a D strip to the other side of the C strip. You should now have a pieced set, 4½" (11.5 cm) wide.

3 Repeat step 2 until you have six sets of pieced strips. **PRESS** all the seam allowances *toward the darker fabrics (p. 41)*. Cut the strips, perpendicular to the seams, into 4½" (11.5 cm) squares. You should be able to cut at least nine squares from each set; you will need a total of 48 squares to make the wall hanging.

4 Stitch two squares, right sides together, in vertical-horizontal arrangement, with the darkest strips at the right and top. Press the seam allowances toward the vertical dark strip.

5 Stitch two more squares, right sides together, in horizontal-vertical arrangement, with the darkest strips at the top and right. Press the seam allowances toward the vertical light strip.

TIP Be sure to keep the fabrics in the same sequence from left to right and top to bottom throughout the quilt.

6 Stitch the two sets, right sides together and seams aligned. *Insert a pin in the wells of the seams (p. 41),* to make sure they line up exactly. Stitch them together, removing the pins as you come to them and keeping the seam allowances turned in the opposite directions. Press the seam allowance toward the lower set.
CONTINUED

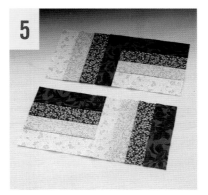

CONTINUED

7 Repeat steps 4 to 6 until you have assembled 12 identical blocks. Arrange them in four rows of three blocks, on a flat surface. Stitch each horizontal row of blocks together, matching the seams and keeping the seam allowances turned in the direction they were pressed. Press the seam allowances in the top and third rows toward one side; press the seam allowances in the second and fourth rows in the opposite direction (note arrows). Return them to the flat surface.

8 Place the top two rows right sides together, aligning seams. Insert pins in the wells of the seams to make sure they line up exactly. Stitch them together, removing the pins as you come to them and keeping the seam allowances turned in opposite directions. Press the seam allowances toward the lower row. Continue until you have stitched all four rows together.

TIP Press the quilt top lightly from the right side and then return it to the flat surface. Now, stand back and let your eyes play for a while over the nifty zigzag pattern you have created.

9 Cut four 1½" (3.8 cm) strips from the entire crosswise width of fabric C, for the inner border. *Measure the quilt top across the middle (p. 29).* Cut two of the border strips equal to this measurement. Pin one strip to the top of the quilt; pin the other strip to the bottom. Align the ends of the strips to the outer edges of the quilt top. Stretch the strips or the quilt slightly, if necessary, to make them fit. Stitch ¼" (6 mm) seams; press the seam allowances toward the borders.

10 Measure the quilt top down the middle. Cut the two side border strips equal to this measurement. Pin a strip to each side of the quilt, aligning the ends of the strips to the edges of the quilt top. Stretch the strips or the quilt slightly, if necessary, to make them fit. Stitch ¼" (6 mm) seams; press the seam allowances toward the borders.

11 Cut four 2½" (6.5 cm) strips from the entire crosswise width of fabric D, for the outer border. Measure for and apply the outer borders in the same manner as the inner borders.

12 Cut the backing fabric and batting 4" (10 cm) longer and wider than the quilt top. Layer and baste the quilt (page 20). Attach a walking foot. Quilt by stitching in the ditch (page 27), *following this sequence (p. 43):* Begin with a diagonal path near the center, stitching along both sides of the darkest zigzagging strip. Then stitch around both border seams. Finish quilting the remaining zigzagging strips. Bind the quilt (page 28).

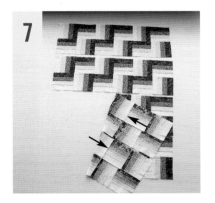

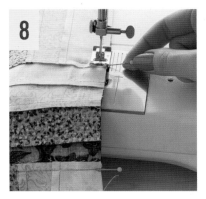

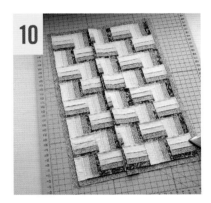

Churn Dash **WALL HANGING**

The simple nine-patch blocks of this Amish-style quilt are made of squares, rectangles, and triangles. The design, symbolic of the mixing movements of an antique butter churn, is created in black fabric and set off by solid, bold, background colors. The triple border frames the design to perfection. Continuous diagonal quilting lines trace the outer corners of all the churn dash blocks and keep the eye moving over the surface of the quilt.

WHAT YOU'LL LEARN

How to piece a nine-patch block using a variety of shapes

How to separate blocks with sashing

How to sew a quilt with multiple borders

How to mark quilting lines on a quilt top

WHAT YOU'LL NEED

⅝ yd. (0.6 m) black fabric for churn dash design and second border

¼ yd. (0.25 m) each of three background fabrics

1⅓ yd. (1.27 m) for sashing, first and third borders, and binding

Rotary cutter and mat

Quilting ruler

Marking pencil

1⅛ yd. (1.05 m) muslin for backing

Low-loft batting, about 38" (96.5 cm) square

Thread to match or blend with the fabrics

How to Sew a CHURN DASH WALL HANGING

LET'S BEGIN

1 Straighten the cut edges of the fabrics and trim off the **SELVAGES** (page 13). Cut two 2⅞" (7.2 cm) strips on the **CROSSWISE GRAIN** of the black fabric. From the strips, cut 18 2⅞" (7.2 cm) squares. Cut the squares in half diagonally to make 36 triangles. Also from the black fabric, cut two 2½" (6.5 cm) strips on the crosswise grain. From the strips, cut 36 1½" × 2½" (3.8 × 6.5 cm) rectangles. (You may have to cut a few of the rectangles from strips left over after cutting the squares.)

2 Cut 36 triangles and 36 rectangles from the background fabrics (12 of each color) in the same sizes as the black ones cut in step 1. Cut three 2½" (6.5 cm) squares from each of the background colors for the centers of the blocks.

3 Cut seven 2½" (6.5 cm) strips on the crosswise grain for the **SASHING** and first border. Cut one strip into six 6½" (16.5 cm) pieces for vertical sashing. From

the same fabric, cut four 3½" (9 cm) strips on the crosswise grain for the third border and four 3" (7.5 cm) strips for binding. Cut four 1½" (3.8 cm) strips on the crosswise grain of the black fabric for the second border.

4 Place one design and one background triangle, right sides together, aligning all the edges. Stitch ¼" (6 mm) from the long edge, taking care not to stretch the **BIAS** edges. Repeat for the remaining 35 pairs, **CHAINSTITCHING** one right after the other, without cutting the thread.

5 Place one design and one background rectangle, right sides together, aligning all the edges. Stitch ¼" (6 mm) from one long edge. Repeat for the remaining 35 rectangle pairs, chainstitching one right after the other, without cutting the thread.

6 Clip the triangle and rectangle pairs apart. **PRESS** the seam allowances *toward the black fabric (p. 41)*. Trim off the points that extend beyond the corners of the triangle-pieced squares. CONTINUED

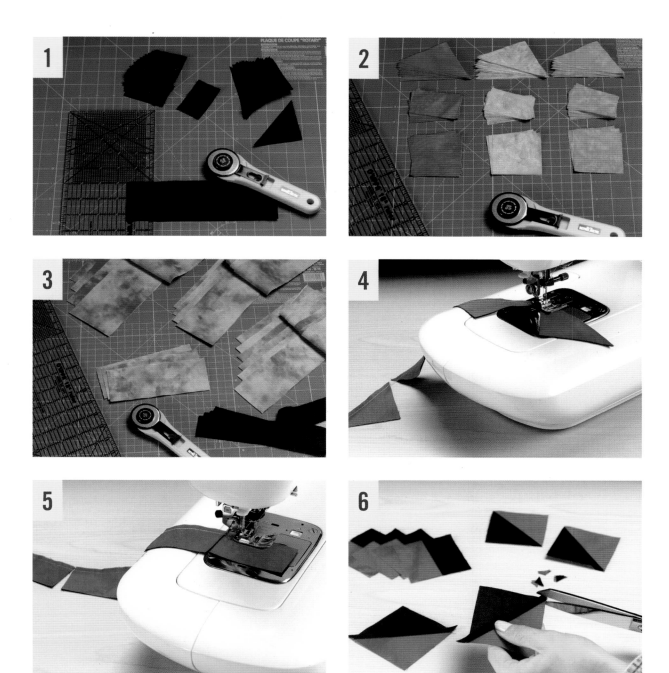

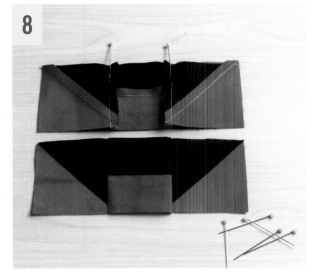

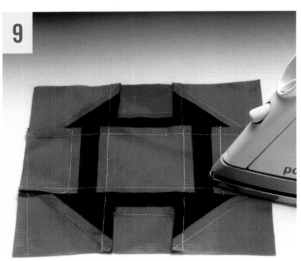

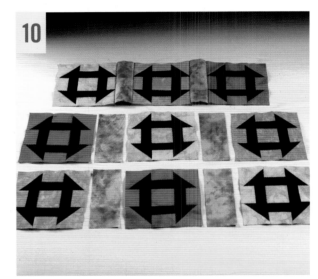

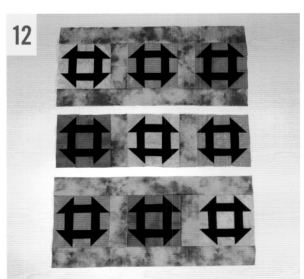

How to Sew a CHURN DASH WALL HANGING

CONTINUED

7 Arrange the eight pieced squares around the plain center square for each block as shown. Stitch each row of blocks together. **FINGER-PRESS** the seam allowances of the top and bottom rows toward the center. Finger-press the seam allowances of the center row away from the center.

TIP Clip thread short at the beginning and end of each seam as you go along. This will keep the back of the block looking much neater and prevent long thread tails from getting caught up in the seams.

8 Place the top row over the middle row, right sides together, aligning the edges and seams. The seam allowances will be pressed in opposite directions. *Insert a pin in the wells of the seams (p. 41),* to make sure they line up exactly. Stitch the rows together, *removing the pins as you come to them (p. 31)* and keeping the seam allowances turned in the opposite directions. Stitch the

bottom row to the other side of the middle row in the same manner.

TIP As you approach seam allowances that have been pressed toward the presser foot, the raw edges may "buckle" under the front of the presser foot. Stop stitching with the needle down in the fabric, and raise the presser foot to allow the seam allowances to return to their pressed position. Use a long pin or the point of your seam ripper to coax them into place and hold them there while you lower the presser foot and continue stitching.

9 Repeat steps 7 and 8 for the remaining eight blocks. Press the blocks, turning the long seam allowances away from the middle.

10 Arrange the blocks on a surface in three rows of three blocks, following the photo on page 56 or in an order of your own choosing. Place short sashing strips between the blocks in each row. Stitch the first row of sashing strips and blocks together, keeping the pieces in their arranged order. Align the ends of the strips to the

upper and lower edges of the blocks, easing the blocks to fit as necessary. It is easiest to stitch with the sashing strip on top, keeping the seam allowances of the block turned in the direction they were pressed.

11 Repeat step 10 for the middle and bottom rows. Check to make sure that the outer points of the black triangles just touch the sashing. If any points are not right, remove the stitches for about 1" (2.5 cm) on each sides of the point, using the point of a seam ripper, and restitch them with the block on top so you can be sure the new stitching line intersects with the point. Press all the seam allowances toward the sashing strips.

12 Return the rows to the work surface. Measure the rows. Cut two sashing strips and two inner border strips to the length of the shortest row. Pin the top border to the top of the top row, easing in fullness evenly. Stitch. Add the sashing to the bottom of the top row. Stitch a border and a sashing strip to the top and bottom of the bottom row. CONTINUED

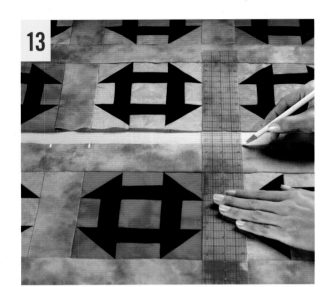

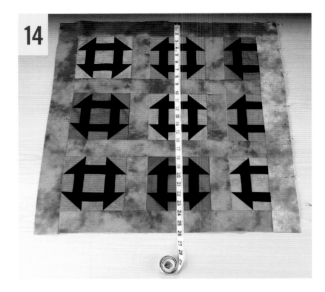

How to Sew a CHURN DASH WALL HANGING

CONTINUED

13 Place a straightedge along the first seam between the sashing and block of the top row, extending across the sashing. Make a small mark on the unstitched edge of the sashing next to the straightedge. Repeat at each seam. Pin the middle row to the upper sashing, making sure that the seams align to the marks. Stitch. Join the lower row to the middle row in the same manner.

14 Check the points as in step 11. Correct any that are not perfect. Press the seam allowances toward the sashing and borders. Measure down the center of the quilt and cut the side borders to this length. Pin in place and

stitch. Press seam allowances toward the borders.

15 Cut second border strips equal in length to the measurement across the middle of the quilt. Attach the top and bottom borders; press allowances toward the second border. Cut the side borders equal in length to the measurement down the center of the quilt. Attach the side borders; press seam allowances toward the second border.

16 Repeat step 15 for the third border. Spread the quilt out on a flat surface. If you have stitched accurately, the diagonal lines of the churn dash corners will align diagonally across the quilt. You can easily "eyeball" the quilting path in the area of the blocks. Align

a straightedge to one of the diagonal lines and, using a quilt marking pencil, mark the lines extending over the borders. Repeat for the other diagonals in all directions.

17 Layer and baste the quilt as on page 20. Attach a walking foot. Thread the machine with thread that matches the outer border. Machine-quilt by stitching in the ditch (page 27) of all the border seams. Then stitch along the horizontal sashings. When you quilt the vertical sashings, cross to the opposite side over the horizontal sashings, forming an X at the block corners. Finish by quilting the diagonal lines. Bind the edges, following the directions on page 28.

15

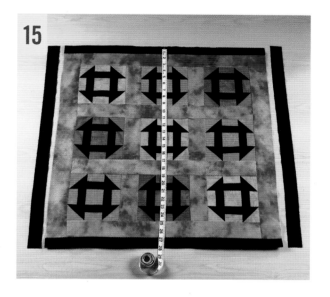

16

17

GLOSSARY

APPLIQUÉ. This French word refers to a decoration or cutout that is applied to the surface of a larger piece of fabric. Many methods of appliqué are used, including simply machine stitching around the outline of the decoration or hand stitching invisibly.

BIAS refers to the diagonal direction of a piece of fabric. True bias is at a 45° angle to both the lengthwise and crosswise grains. Woven fabric has the greatest amount of stretch on the bias.

CHAINSTITCHING. Sewing several individual seams without breaking the stitching threads between the pieces, thus saving time and trips to the ironing board.

COLOR VALUE refers to the relative lightness or darkness of a fabric. In selecting fabrics for a quilt project, it is often necessary to evaluate the color values of various fabrics, both solid colors and prints.

CROSSWISE GRAIN. On woven fabric, the crosswise grain runs perpendicular to the selvages. Fabric has slight "give" in the crosswise grain.

FAT QUARTERS. A half-yard (0.5 m) of fabric, cut down the middle to measure 18" x 22" (46 x 56 cm). This is the equivalent of a quarter-yard (0.25 m) of fabric.

FINGER-PRESS. Rather than use an iron, seam allowances are temporarily pressed to one side with the fingers. This is usually done for bias seams to avoid distortion.

GLUE STICK. This temporary fabric adhesive in a plastic tube is a convenient substitute for pinning or basting when you need to hold fabric in place temporarily before stitching. The glue can be applied in small dots. It won't discolor the fabric and can be washed out. It will not harm

your machine or gum up your needle as you stitch.

GRAINLINE. Woven fabrics have two grainlines. The lengthwise grainline runs parallel to the selvages. It is the strongest direction of the fabric with the least amount of "give." The crosswise grainline runs perpendicular to the selvages and will "give" slightly when pulled.

LENGTHWISE GRAIN. On woven fabric, the lengthwise grain runs parallel to the selvages. It is the strongest direction of the fabric with the least amount of "give."

LOFT refers to the thickness and springiness of the batting.

MUSLIN. Often used for quilt backings and sleeves on wall hangings or for light background areas in patchwork quilts, this mediumweight, plain-weave cotton fabric is relatively inexpensive. Unbleached muslin is off-white with tiny brown flecks; bleached muslin is white.

PIVOT. Perfect corners are stitched by stopping with the needle down in the fabric at the exact corner, before turning the fabric. To be sure the corner stitch locks, turn the handwheel until the needle goes all the way down and just begins to rise.

PRESSING. This step is extremely important to the success of your quilting projects. Select the heat setting appropriate for your fabric and use steam. Lift and lower the iron in an overlapping pattern. Do not slide the iron down the seam, as this can cause the fabric to stretch out of shape, especially on the crosswise grain or bias.

QUILTING HOOP. Similar to an embroidery hoop, this circular or oval, two-piece wooden frame holds the quilt layers taut while you are

hand-quilting. An adjustable screw allows you to tighten or loosen the outer hoop to accommodate various thicknesses without crushing the quilt.

QUILTING TEMPLATE. A simple, rigid shape is used as a guide for tracing design lines onto the quilt top for machine or hand quilting. Templates can be cut from firm card stock or translucent vinyl. Ready-made vinyl templates and quilting stencils, also used for marking designs, can be purchased at quilt shops.

SASHING. Strips of fabric, plain or pieced, that are sewn between the square block units of a quilt.

SEAM. Two pieces of fabric are placed right sides together and joined along the edge with stitches. After stitching, the raw edges are hidden on the inside, leaving a clean, smooth line on the outside.

SEAM ALLOWANCE. Excess fabric which lies between the stitching line and the raw edge. Stitching with a narrow $1/4$" (6 mm) seam allowance is traditional for quilting projects because it minimizes the bulk of fabric behind narrow strips and points.

SELVAGE. Characteristic of woven fabrics, this narrow, tightly woven outer edge should be cut away. Avoid the temptation to use it as one edge of a quilting piece, as it may cause seams to pucker and it may shrink excessively when washed.

STRIP PIECING. Creating pieced designs from long strips of fabric by stitching the strips together and then cutting them crosswise. This method saves time over cutting each piece individually and then sewing them together.